Angel
Answers

Angel
Answers

A Celestial Oracle

Juan Nakamori
Translated by Akiko Fujinami

Red Wheel
Boston, MA / York Beach, ME

This edition first published in 2005 by
Red Wheel/Weiser, LLC
York Beach, ME
With offices at:
368 Congress Street
Boston, MA 02210
www.redwheelweiser.com

Library of Congress Cataloging-in-Publication Data
Nakamori, Juan.
[Angel messages]
Angel answers: a celestial oracle / Juan Nakamori ; translated by
Akiko Fujinami.
p. cm.
Originally published: Angel messages. London: Rider, 2004.
ISBN 1-59003-092-3
1. Fortune-telling by books. I. Title.

BF1891.B66N35 2005
133.3'3--dc22
2005050410

Typeset in Perpetua and Wade Sans by Kathleen Wilson Fivel

Printed in Canada
Friesens

12 11 10 09 08 07 06 05
8 7 6 5 4 3 2 1

How to Awaken
Your Inner Angel

1. Hold the closed book, shut your eyes and become aware of your breathing.

2. Gradually calm your thoughts and, as you relax, focus on your question or problem.

3. Send your question out into the universe and wait.

4. Whichever number between 1 and 174 first comes to you, open that page and study the message on it. This is your answer.

You are born with love.

You are blessed to live with love.

2

Nothing happens by coincidence.

Every single event is designed

to guide you toward inner awakening

and true happiness.

3

Be as open hearted

as an innocent child.

Your potential will infinitely increase.

4

Trust that whatever you truly need will

be given to you at the right moment.

Believe in this Universal Law and enjoy

every aspect of your endeavour.

5

Remember that you create your own

reality. Whatever you do, create

harmony in yourself first.

6

You may choose to judge things as right or wrong, and as superior or inferior. But the Universe accepts all matters as they are, for what they are.

7

Focus on the challenge in hand.
As you sincerely and diligently
carry out your task, it will change
in the process.

8

Be confident, and love and nourish yourself. You are gifted with all the ability, charm and energy you need.

9

Gentleness heals and strengthens your body and mind. Gentleness embraces and rejuvenates the bodies and minds of those around you.

Consider each matter with clarity and insight. Let light and radiance flow through your thoughts.

Will you diminish yourself by

competing and comparing yourself

with others? Or will you increase your

joy by praising them?

12

Stop thinking for a while and allow
yourself to feel. Your feelings will
reveal much more than thoughts
alone could explain.

13

Be grateful for every single thing, for

every person and for all of existence.

Your heart-felt gratitude will create a

pathway toward happiness.

14

As long as you continue to blame others, the truth will never be revealed to you. When you calmly observe yourself, you will awaken to reality.

15

Trust in the divine nature of your

Inner Self. Free yourself from your

self-imposed restrictions and consider

your infinite potential in life.

16

Tidy up your surroundings and try to live simply. Your problems will gradually disappear with the clutter, allowing you to journey unburdened through life.

17

As you free yourself from attachment,

you will be freed from pain.

Believe in your potential and

rise to the challenge to change.

18

Take part in activities that interest you,

that you enjoy and in which

you can immerse yourself.

Enjoying yourself in this way

will water the flower of your soul.

19

Life is the eternal flow of 'Now'.

Feel the essence of Now

and live in the Now.

20

Try to have a closer relationship with yourself than with anyone else. Real love means learning to cherish your own thoughts and feelings.

21

The Universe yearns to bless you

with innumerable gifts.

It is only waiting for you to open

your heart to receive them.

22

Every person is free to choose. You yourself choose whether to experience joy or pain, to be happy or unhappy.

23

Enjoy visualizing how you would like

your life to be. The more vivid your

dream, the greater the chance

of its coming true.

24

To blame others is to blame yourself.

To blame yourself is to blame others.

25

Self-righteousness and prejudice will

not afford you real insight into the

matter. Open your mind and be brave

enough to communicate.

True love means giving without

demands or expectations.

True love means accepting without

judgement or restraint.

27

Take a good long look at something

that may seem small and insignificant.

Therein lies a big message.

28

Each and every emotion offers
lessons to help you get to know
your Inner Self. Do not reject or
detest your emotions, but accept
and experience them fully.

29

Allow the Universe to love you, to guide you and to support you. Always keep the door of your heart wide open.

You are not expected to suffer any

hardship that you cannot overcome.

Instead of attempting to escape from

your problems, accept them calmly and

try to resolve them.

31

Do not waste your energy on that

which is unworthy of you. Live fully in

this precious moment with joy.

Be as free as the wind and yet as strong

as a mountain! Expand your horizons

as infinitely as the sky, with the

playfulness of a bird!

33

Your reality is a mirror that reflects your Inner Self. Observe it carefully and discover yourself.

34

As you free yourself from attachment,

you will gain spontaneity.

As you remove restrictions,

you will gain freedom.

Relax and tune into the harmonious

rhythms of Nature. Impatience

and aggressive action may well

cause stagnation.

36

Treasure animals and plants.

Love them in the same way

that you love your friends.

It is often easy to blame,

but difficult to forgive. And yet,

although it may be hard, forgiveness

is surely always worth trying.

38

Imagination is a seed of creation that blooms like a flower. Visualize a detailed picture of the flower that you would like to bloom.

39

Whatever it is, try to accept it with a

'Thank you!' That way, it will become

yet one more of life's blessings!

Birds fly in the sky without worry and flowers bloom without fear. Nature is a treasure trove of such good examples, offering lessons for us all.

41

Live with enduring trust and hope.

Your Angel will always light your way.

If you would like a significant wish to come true, start with several smaller wishes first. If you have plans and dreams for the future, begin by treasuring today.

43

You are born with so much potential.

But, if you say to yourself, 'This is all

I have', indeed this is all you have.

44

Every person has inner goodness and beauty. Every event holds a valuable lesson and a beautiful experience within it.

45

Instead of sticking to your opinions

stubbornly, open your mind gracefully.

As your thoughts change, your

situation will also change.

46

Cheer up others with your wit
and charm. Encourage them
with kind words.

47

Release tension from your body and mind, and relax. Take a deep breath and communicate with your Inner Light.

48

Accept small problems with a smile

and allow them to fade away.

Remain open minded in order

to accomplish large tasks.

49

Will you stay where you are now,

fearful of losing your security

and comfort? Or, wishing to make

true progress, will you take

a brave step forward?

50

Offer your heart-felt gratitude to the

invisible Source of love and guidance.

You will always receive help

from this unseen power.

51

Accept all your emotions consciously,

without being swayed by them.

Taste each emotion fully, but

without over-indulging yourself.

52

Everything that you send out into the
world will come back to you. For you
yourself create your own signs in order
that you might begin to know yourself.

53

If there is a problem, face it calmly.

Rather than seeking a hasty solution,

consider your situation objectively.

There are so many different paths

that you could follow. You just have

to choose the one that's right

for you, take a step forward

and then keep walking.

55

If you have been grasping onto

something, try to let it go.

Your empty hands will be ready to

receive a new gift.

Do not complicate matters by thinking too much about them. The truth is really very simple.

Be as beautiful as a flower in a field.

Be as joyous as a bird flying in the sky.

58

Do not worry about what others

think of you. People will always believe

whatever they want.

59

Everyone lives life in his or her unique

way. Live your life honouring

your own unique way.

60

Be gentle toward all living things.

Every single life is your companion,

your friend and your teacher.

61

Always keep your body, mind and soul

open. Angelic guidance will come to

you in the form of your intuition.

62

Do not be weighed down by past failures, blunders or errors.

For it is these experiences that will lead you toward the opportunity to achieve your goal.

63

Everyone is born with a unique

personality and a mission in life. Yours

will flourish if you use your positive

characteristics and your talents.

Try not to be affected by the words

and attitudes of others. Instead,

calmly consider your own

words and attitudes.

65

Set your priorities according to the
importance and urgency of whatever
faces you. Do not neglect
what you must do now.

66

Enjoy, appreciate and learn from the diversity of the four seasons. Likewise, enjoy and appreciate every phase of your own life, savouring its richness.

67

Happiness will never come to you

from the outside. Not unless you

open wide the door of your heart.

68

Be brave enough to do what you really want to do. Do whatever you enjoy with enough conviction and you will find success.

69

As you look up at the sky,

be aware of the blanket of benevolence

spread above you. As you gently

close your eyes, know that blessings

are raining down upon you.

70

Carefully observe the minor details of
your life. In your daily life lies every seed
necessary for your spiritual growth.

71

Open your mind and try to face

that person. Calm your mind

and try to talk to yourself.

72

Your tenderness is the warmth of a

spring sun. Your tenderness is

the fragrance of a flower

blooming in the desert.

73

Think about what you are holding

on to. Therein lies the root of your

problems and pain.

74

Inspiration is a gift from the Source of

love. Do not dam its flow with

thoughts and judgements.

75

Be generous and open-minded when

considering the business of others.

Be meticulous about your own affairs

and consider them carefully.

Observe every aspect of the world.

In doing so, you will discover every

aspect of yourself.

Love forgives everything, including

failure, error, betrayal and hatred.

Love heals everything, including

discomfort, fear, pain and loneliness.

Flowers are the stars of the earth and birds are earth's Angels. Every single life is a manifestation of great love.

Being dedicated to someone close to
you is the same as being dedicated to
yourself. Serving a stranger is the same
as serving the great Universe.

The source of every emotion resides within you. No other person is able to force emotions upon you.

81

Say 'Thank you' promptly and
open-heartedly. Enjoy the warmth of
love offered to you.

82

Offer your sincere gratitude

to your ancestors, parents and family.

Gratitude to those close to you

is a good starting point on the

road to happiness.

83

Life is studded with innumerable

opportunities. There is no one who is

not blessed with these gifts.

84

A mind that asks for the moon creates
dissatisfaction and pain. A mind that
cherishes what it already has invites
fulfilment and blessings.

85

Flowing water is free of stagnation,

remaining fresh. Drifting clouds are free

of attachment, remaining at liberty.

86

Your mission in life changes according

to the level of your inner growth.

Your current mission is to do as much

as you are capable of doing now.

87

Asking without giving invites

dissatisfaction. Giving without asking

leads to contentment.

88

Trust all to the Universal laws and to

your own infinite potential.

The ultimate outcome will always be

for the Highest Good.

89

Regardless of any excuses you make,

you can never deceive yourself. Be

brave and listen to your Inner Voice.

90

Many things are destined to fade

away, to decay or to disappear.

Seek eternal things that never fade

away or disappear.

91

Do not fret about minor conflicts or mistakes. The important thing is to allow yourself to be as useful as possible in the circumstances.

Live your life honestly and energetically. Never subjugate yourself to the will of others against your better judgement and never live dishonestly.

93

Wisdom and ability flourish through

acts of love. Fill your thoughts,

actions and words with love.

94

Live simply and humbly.

Live in the awareness that

there are many things you just

do not know or understand.

95

If you want to be powerful, be spontaneous. Allow yourself to merge, without pretension or over-exertion, with the flow of Nature.

96

Help will be granted to the soul that
seeks truth. New tasks and blessings
will be bestowed on the soul that
strives to make progress.

97

If you act with unwillingness and from obligation, fatigue and dissatisfaction will be your harvest. If you act with hope and enthusiasm, accomplishment and growth will be your fruits.

98

Treat yourself more gently. Listen to

that inner whisper urging you to be

gentle with yourself.

99

When you talk ceaselessly, time flows away mercilessly. When you listen calmly, a wonderful awakening occurs.

Patience nourishes you with confidence and compassion. But, in order to receive these gifts, patience must be combined with willingness.

101

Jealousy and attachment do not

resonate with the vibration of the

Source of love. Understanding and

tolerance are at one with the Source.

102

Absorb love and energy from
the sun into your body and mind.
Let tenderness and strength shine
into your daily life.

103

A mind that condemns and criticizes diminishes your potential. A mind that is humble, open and flexible increases your capability.

104

Disappointment is a common
companion in life. Your life will
take shape according to how you
react to it.

105

Everyone has his or her own values,

yet there is only one Truth.

That which we value reveals the level

of our spiritual growth.

106

Accept yourself as you are now.

Accept others as they are now.

107

No one else is able to cause you pain.

Heal the cause of your pain by

embracing love.

108

Everyone has curious character quirks.

Try to view each person as objectively

and compassionately as possible.

109

This is your only life and you will never

be able to repeat it. Cherish and live

each day of your life fully, with delight.

Even amidst chaos and in times of

trouble, remain calm and composed.

Instead of angrily doling out blame,

try to offer gentle encouragement.

Do this regardless of whether you are

dealing with yourself or others.

Do not regret what has already been done. Pour your love and strength into whatever lies ahead of you.

113

Respect each glimmer of intuition

that sparks within you.

Treasure all the signs that your

Guardian Angel sends to you.

114

Get to know yourself properly first.

If you do not know yourself,

you will not be able to know

others or Divinity.

115

No matter what your circumstances
are, do not resist them but befriend
them. No matter what a person
is like, do not reject him or her,
but pass on your love.

116

As long as you cannot forgive,

your pain will stay with you.

Uplift your mind, and embrace all.

117

Remember, you were born to be happy.

Keep faith in this and move on.

118

You are never alone.

The Creator's love is always with you,

deep within you.

119

Confidence means trusting completely in your own potential. Freedom means loosening yourself from your own restrictions.

120

You cannot grasp mere illusions

no matter how desperately you

visualize or crave for them.

You must visualize hope instead,

and face reality courageously.

121

You have already been given all that

you need. As you begin to make

proper and joyous use of this,

you will receive even more.

122

Loss creates an opportunity to receive

many things. Within the pain of loss

lies all-encompassing compassion.

123

By yourself, you could not create a

single hair or a single finger.

Your abilities are granted to you by

the love and power of the Creator.

124

Instead of considering a matter from

your single viewpoint, try to observe it

from the perspective of others.

Instead of worrying only about

your own interests, consider the

well-being of the whole.

125

Negative thoughts attract

negative events. Positive thoughts

invite positive events.

Consider whether a particular

problem or pattern keeps repeating

itself in your life. If it does, this is the

voice of your Inner Self, calling you

again and again to wake up.

127

Fate is not what governs you.

Fate is what you choose and

create for yourself.

You can only do as much as you

can do now. Trust the rest to the

wisdom of Nature.

129

Treasure every precious encounter.

To treasure your relationships is

to treasure your life.

130

Discover the brilliance within yourself.

In so doing, you will unearth the

brilliance in every person you meet.

131

Your thoughts, words and actions

will always return to you.

Like an echo, they will come

back to you straight away.

You have chosen your parents,

brothers and sisters. You have chosen

your fate, your destiny and your

physical body.

133

Do not worry about the results of all the efforts you have made. Be grateful and happy with yourself for having done the best you can.

134

Do you spend your time

reminiscing about the past,

or worrying about the future?

Live truly and fully in this moment.

135

Try not to withhold your feelings for fear of getting hurt. If you express them with love, you will create an opportunity for better understanding.

No matter how difficult your
circumstances, never give up hope.
Trust in the wisdom of the
Creator as, out of the blue,
events may turn in your favor.

Do not shy away from the dark clouds

of your mind, but accept them and try

to understand them. They have

appeared for good reason.

Stop being so serious, and try to be

more cheerful and playful!

Stop being so strict, and try

to be more soft and gentle!

139

Create a space for pure and

earnest prayer. Your prayer will

be a stream of light, reaching to

where the Angels are.

140

Carefully cleanse your mind's eye

of clouds and impurities.

Then, goodness, beauty and

truthfulness will be revealed to you.

141

Only through seeing yourself reflected

in others will you be able to know

yourself and grow. Only through

your relationships with others will

you be able to improve yourself

and live life fully.

142

Spare a moment in which to relax.

Use this moment's calm to open

yourself to flashes of inspiration.

143

Do not worry about your age,

the depth of your knowledge or

the breadth of your experiences.

Celestial guidance comes to all

those who crave it.

144

Free your mind from attachment to limited plans and schemes. As you do so, new ideas will come to you from the great Source of love.

145

Innocence is not only a gift for children. Innocence is to be even more treasured as you grow.

Spite, displeasure, obtrusiveness and stubbornness. These are all expressions of minds that crave love.

147

You are a part of the entire Universe.

You are at one with

the entire Universe.

148

Do not be troubled even if you
discover your baser instincts, but
encourage them to follow the example
of your Higher Self. In the school of
life, the baser instincts are students and
the Higher Self their teacher.

149

'Life' means acknowledging this very

moment. 'Love' means living in this

very moment.

150

Increase your courage and love, and
accept all. The Universal Law is based
in complete acceptance.

151

Do not worry about your past,

regardless of how hard it has been.

Start a new life right now

with fresh resolve.

If you act with uncertainty, you will produce uncertain results. If you act with confidence, you will receive the support of the Universe.

153

Even if things do not go quite as you would like them to, do not worry. In order to achieve a balance, carry on with joy and enthusiasm, anticipating the outcome with a peaceful mind.

154

Embrace the warmth of the sun with
your entire body and soul. Your body
and soul will be filled with light,
strength and love.

155

Do not be afraid to reveal yourself.

You will be rewarded with true

freedom, like a naked child

swimming in the ocean.

156

Friendships form part of your life, the essence of who you are — your mind and your body. To treasure your friends is to treasure yourself.

157

Close your eyes lightly and breathe
calmly. Feel how loved you are.

As long as you choose to blame

others or your circumstances,

you will never find happiness.

For it is your soul that has chosen

to experience all these problems.

159

Great joy can be found even

in the tiniest thing that could fit into

the palm of your hand. Sense it

through the Inner Light that resides

deep within you.

Forgive and love yourself

unconditionally. Forgive and love every

other person unconditionally.

161

Do not be swayed by the thoughts of others nor worry about the opinion that others may have of you. Believe in yourself and stay true to yourself.

As you strive hard to master one thing, you will spontaneously be able to understand many others. An enquiring mind provides wings with which to soar freely.

163

You do not need to grieve over your inabilities or weaknesses. Your mission in life is to display your unique qualities and strengths.

164

Within every situation, brightness can
be found. Within every person,
Divinity shines.

165

You are a child of the great

Source of love. You are blessed

to live in great love.

166

Uncertainty, fear, worry and hatred are illusions created by your mind. They will disappear through gratitude, trust, compassion and devotion.

167

The Universal Law supports you

according to the needs of your soul.

Every event supports and nourishes the

growth of your soul.

168

Observe how you project yourself

onto every person and every situation.

Self-knowledge opens

the door to truth.

169

Your physical body will disappear one

day. Seek to know your soul,

which enjoys eternal life.

Each and every moment brings with it

the opportunity to create a new self.

Live in this present moment and be

open-minded.

Any negative can be changed

to a positive. The power to

transform negatives into positives

is inherently yours.

After a storm, the sun shines forth brightly —— such is the wisdom of the Universe. After an ordeal, the soul shines forth brilliantly —— such are the blessings of the Universe.

173

Fill your thoughts with brightness and serenity. Therein lies the key to your spiritual progress.

174

You are protected this very moment,
always and forever. Take comfort in this
and live your life in harmony with your
Higher Self.

EPILOGUE

As the title of this book suggests, I am not the true author of these messages, which came to me in sudden flashes of inspiration. When I received them, I had to stop thinking, empty myself and tune in to the Universe. You could say that I received the messages as inner vibrations, which I then tried to express in words. Even though I do not practice any particular religion or follow one spiritual path, I feel truly grateful that I have been able to share this gift, which spontaneously appeared in my life, with you.

Our amazing Universe supports the existence of every creature on earth. Its nurturing care means that we are empowered and blessed with the elements and lessons necessary for our individual growth. In this respect, the message that you have chosen intuitively in this book may be one that your Higher Self wishes to send to you.

About the Author

Juan Nakamori was born in Tokyo, Japan. Looking up at the sky one night, she had a vision of a multitude of angels filling the heavens. Since then, the angel messages that she has received have filled readers around the world with love and encouragement, offering them healing and enlightenment. She has published a number of best-selling books drawing upon this celestial wisdom.

To Our Readers

Red Wheel, an imprint of Red Wheel/Weiser, publishes books on topics ranging from spunky self-help, spirituality, personal growth, and relationships to women's issues and social issues. Our mission is to publish quality books that will make a difference in people's lives—how we feel about ourselves and how we relate to one another and to the world at large. We value integrity, compassion, and receptivity, both in the books we publish and in the way we do business.

Our readers are our most important resource, and we value your input, suggestions, and ideas about what you would like to see published. Please feel free to contact us, to request our latest book catalog, or to be added to our mailing list.

Red Wheel/Weiser, LLC
P.O. Box 612
York Beach, ME 03910–0612
www.redwheelweiser.com